Learning to Read, Step by Step!

Ready to Read **Preschool–Kindergarten**
• big type and easy words • rhyme and rhythm • picture clues
For children who know the alphabet and are eager to
begin reading.

Reading with Help **Preschool–Grade 1**
• basic vocabulary • short sentences • simple stories
For children who recognize familiar words and sound out
new words with help.

Reading on Your Own **Grades 1–3**
• engaging characters • easy-to-follow plots • popular topics
For children who are ready to read on their own.

Reading Paragraphs **Grades 2–3**
• challenging vocabulary • short paragraphs • exciting stories
For newly independent readers who read simple sentences
with confidence.

Ready for Chapters **Grades 2–4**
• chapters • longer paragraphs • full-color art
For children who want to take the plunge into chapter books
but still like colorful pictures.

STEP INTO READING® is designed to give every child a successful
reading experience. The grade levels are only guides; children will progress
through the steps at their own speed, developing confidence in their reading.
The F&P Text Level on the back cover serves as another tool to help you
choose the right book for your child.

Remember, a lifetime love of reading starts with a single step!

In memory of my mother
and the orphan she loved
—M.K.

To Mom and Dad
—V.F.

With grateful acknowledgment to the kind people at the Schuyler Mansion State Historic Site, New York State Parks, Recreation & Historic Preservation, in Albany, New York, for their time and expertise in reviewing this book.

Text copyright © 2018 by Monica Kulling
Cover art and interior illustrations copyright © 2018 by Valerio Fabbretti

Visit us on the Web!
StepIntoReading.com
rhcbooks.com

Educators and librarians, for a variety of teaching tools, visit us at RHTeachersLibrarians.com

Library of Congress Cataloging-in-Publication Data
Names: Kulling, Monica, author. | Fabbretti, Valerio, illustrator.
Title: Eliza Hamilton : founding mother / by Monica Kulling ; illustrated by Valerio Fabbretti.
Description: New York : Random House, 2018. | Series: Step into reading. Step 3
Identifiers: LCCN 2017051119 (print) | LCCN 2017052315 (ebook) |
ISBN 978-1-5247-7234-5 (ebook) | ISBN 978-1-5247-7232-1 (trade pbk.) |
ISBN 978-1-5247-7233-8 (hardcover library binding)
Subjects: LCSH: Hamilton, Elizabeth Schuyler, 1757–1854—Juvenile literature. |
Politicians' spouses—United States—Biography—Juvenile literature. | Hamilton, Alexander, 1757–1804—Family—Juvenile literature.
Classification: LCC E302.6.H22 (ebook) | LCC E302.6.H22 K85 2018 (print) |
DDC 973.4092 [B]—dc23

Printed in the United States of America
10 9 8 7 6 5 4 3

This book has been officially leveled by using the F&P Text Level Gradient™ Leveling System.

Eliza Hamilton
Founding Mother

by Monica Kulling
illustrated by Valerio Fabbretti

Random House 🏠 New York

Elizabeth Schuyler (SKY-ler)
was born in 1757.
Her father was a major general
in the Colonial army
and an important landowner.
Her devoted mother came from
one of the richest families
in New York State.
Eliza would grow up to marry
Alexander Hamilton—
one of America's Founding Fathers.

Few people know about
the *great* things Eliza achieved.
It's time they did!

Eliza grew up in Albany, New York.
She had many brothers and sisters.
They lived in a mansion
called the Pastures,
which stood on a hill
near the Hudson River.

When she was a girl,
Eliza loved to climb trees.
One day she saw her cat
catch a young bird.
"No!" yelled Eliza.

She rescued the bird.

Eliza cared for the little orphan

until it was well enough

to fly again.

Eliza often brought
the outdoors inside.
One day she had something
surprising in her hat.
"Snake!" her sisters screamed.

"Take it outside, Eliza!"
ordered Mama.
"Now!"

At mealtimes,
the family talked about
the news of the day.
One evening in 1775,
Eliza's father announced,
"A shot was fired
in Lexington, Massachusetts."

"What will happen now, Papa?"
asked seventeen-year-old Eliza.
"We will go to war with England,"
said her father.
It was the start
of the American Revolution.

Important people often
ate at the Schuyler home.
Benjamin Franklin visited in 1776.

On a walk with the family,

he saw Eliza scramble up

a steep hill.

"She's a bold soldier," he said.

Eliza was strong.

One day a young soldier
named Alexander Hamilton
came with a message
for Eliza's father.
He stayed for dinner, too.
Alex talked about his many ideas
for making a new nation—
a country not ruled by a king.
General Schuyler listened.
So did Eliza!

The American army
was camped for the winter
near Morristown, New Jersey.

Eliza was staying nearby with
her aunt and uncle.
At a party,
she met Alexander again.
They met many times after.
Soon they grew close.

On December 14, 1780,
Eliza's family stood near
as she and Alex were married.

Alexander was an orphan.

Eliza's large and loving family
welcomed him
as one of their own.

Alex went back to work—
writing letters to Congress
for General George Washington.
But he wanted to fight.
In 1781, he led an attack
at Yorktown, Virginia,
that helped end the war
in the colonies.

Three months later,

back at home,

Eliza gave birth to their first child.

Eliza and Alex had a son.
They named him Philip,
after her father.
Alex came home a hero.
He got work as a lawyer.

In Lower Manhattan,
where the family lived,
Eliza kept busy with
their family.
She also helped Alex
with his political career.

Alex wrote many essays
to convince voters
to accept the Constitution.
Its laws would hold
the states together.

Eliza read what Alex wrote.
Her wise advice helped him
write more clearly.

On April 30, 1789,

George Washington

became the first president

of the United States.

He chose Alex to be the first

secretary of the treasury—

the manager of the money system.

Eliza ran the household.
She was smart about
stretching the little money
that came in.

She had to be—
the Hamilton family
was growing!

Besides her own children,
Eliza had welcomed
two needy children
into her heart and home.
There were many mouths
to feed!

Then tragedy struck.

November 23, 1801

Eliza and Alex's oldest son, Philip,

was nineteen

when he fought a duel.

This was a gunfight

to defend one's honor.

Alex told his son,

"Don't aim to kill."

But the other man shot

to kill.

Philip was dead.

Eliza's heart was broken.

But more losses were to come.

Her second child, Angelica,

broke down at the death

of her favorite brother.

She never recovered.

Angelica would be

under a doctor's care

for the rest of her life.

Eliza had already lost
her sister Peggy.
Then her mother died in 1803.
But perhaps the hardest blow came
on July 11, 1804.
Vice President Aaron Burr didn't like
what Alex wrote and said about him.
Burr challenged him to a duel.

Alex took the advice
he had given his son.
Burr shot to kill.
Alex died the next day.

Eliza prayed to be strong.

She needed to be!

Alexander had left debts.

Their beloved home,

called the Grange,

had to be sold.

A few months after Alex died,

Eliza lost her dear father, too.

He had left her some money.

With it,

she bought back the Grange.

Eliza wanted to make

a difference in the lives

of homeless children.

Her friend Isabella Graham

also had a heart for orphans.

In 1806,

along with a few other women,

they started the

Orphan Asylum Society

of the City of New York.

They raised money

and bought a house

where children without family

could live.

The two-story house in
Greenwich Village, New York City,
was home to sixteen orphans.
But soon the house was too small.
The women raised more money
and built a bigger orphanage.
Eliza was its first vice president.
In 1821,
she became its president.
The orphanage later became
a place that helped children
and families in need,
and it still exists today.

Eliza wanted every child
to know how to read and write.
She also wanted history
to remember her husband.
In 1818,
she opened the first school in
Washington Heights, New York City.
She named it the
Hamilton Free School.

HAMILTON
FREE
SCHOOL

Eliza also raised money

to build a memorial

to honor America's first president.

She joined two former first ladies—

Dolley Madison and Louisa Adams—

in this effort.

The Washington Monument

was finally opened to the public

in 1888,

but not in time for Eliza

to see it in all its glory.

Eliza outlived Alex by fifty years!
She raised their children
and helped so many others.
She organized Alex's writings
for publication
so future generations
would know about him.
She was laid to rest in 1854
beside her beloved Alexander.
Elizabeth Schuyler Hamilton
lived to be ninety-seven years old.